Mario Molina

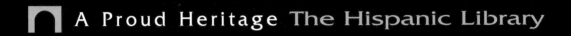

A Proud Heritage The Hispanic Library

Mario Molina

Chemist and Nobel Prize Winner

Deborah Kent

The Child's World®

Published in the United States of America by The Child's World®
PO Box 326 • Chanhassen, MN 55317-0326 • 800-599-READ • www.childsworld.com

Acknowledgments
The Childs World®: Mary Berendes, Publishing Director
Editorial Directions, Inc.: E. Russell Primm, Editorial Director; Pam Rosenberg, Project Editor;
Melissa McDaniel, Line Editor; Katie Marsico, Assistant Editor; Matt Messbarger, Editorial
Assistant; Susan Hindman, Copyeditor; Susan Ashley and Sarah E. De Capua, Proofreaders;
Chris Simms and Olivia Nellums, Fact Checkers; Timothy Griffin/IndexServ, Indexer; Katie
Marsico, Photo Researcher; Linda S. Koutris, Photo Selector
Creative Spark: Mary Francis and Rob Court, Design and Page Production
Cartography by XNR Productions, Inc.

Photos
    Cover: Dr. Mario Molina speaking at a press conference
    Cover photograph: AP/Wide World Photo
    Interior photographs: AP/Wide World Photo: 17, 18, 21, 29, 30, 33; Corbis: 7 (Michael S.
    Lewis), 8 (Michael Maslan Historic Photographs), 9 (Charles & Josette Lenars), 10 (Clouds
    Hill Imaging Ltd.), 12 (Hulton-Deutsch Collection), 15 (Jonathan Blair), 19, 23 (Mark M.
    Lawrence), 24 (Peter Turnley), 25 (Galen Rowell), 26, 27 (Roger Ressmeyer), 28 (Kevin
    Fleming), 31 (Bettmann), 32 (Ted Spiegel), 34 (Colin Garratt; Milepost 92 1/2); Greg
    Smith/Corbis Saba: 22; Kraft Brooks/Corbis Sygma: 16, 35.

Library of Congress Cataloging-in-Publication Data
    Cataloging-in-Publication data for this title has been applied for and is available from the
    United States Library of Congress.

Contents

7   15   26   30

Chapter One

The Chemist in the Bathroom

On a March day in 2002, Dr. Mario Molina and his wife, Luisa, stood before a group of scientists and government officials in Mexico City. They presented their new book, *Air Quality in the Mexico Megacity,* to the admiring audience. The book brought together the ideas of many scientists about how to improve Mexico City's air quality. It included much of Molina's past work and described work that still needed to be done. The audience was very eager to hear what Molina had to say. Few other scientists had done so much to help protect Earth's **atmosphere.** Molina's vital research had already earned him a Nobel Prize, the highest honor a scientist can receive.

Mario Molina was born in Mexico City on March 19, 1943. He was the fourth in a family of seven children. His father, Roberto Molina Pasquel, was a lawyer and taught at the University of Mexico. (The name of the university in Spanish is the Universidad Nacional Autónoma de México, or UNAM.) The Molina family lived in a big, sprawling house with gardens, patios, and balconies. On sunny days, Mario could see two snow-

The air quality in Mexico City is so poor that it affects the health of the people living there. Residents sometimes have a hard time breathing or even suffer from illnesses related to the lack of fresh air.

capped volcanoes, Popocatepetl (poh-puh-KAH-tuh-peh-tel) and Ixtacihuatl (ees-tah-SEE-wah-tel). The mountains looked down on the city like watchful guardians.

As a small child, Mario showed a talent for music. He took lessons on the violin, and his parents thought

Mount Ixtacihuatl overlooks Mexico City and is 17,343 feet (5,286 meters) tall. Ixtacihuatl is an inactive volcano, so it is not likely to erupt any time soon.

The Aztec people of central Mexico once lived in a splendid city called Tenochtitlán (tay-noch-tee-TLAHN) (above). Tenochtitlán stood on the site where Mexico City stands today. The Aztecs believed that the snowcapped volcanoes, Popocatepetl and Ixtacihuatl, were a god and goddess. When the Aztecs heard thunder over the mountains, they thought that the god and goddess were fighting.

Mario Molina's interest in science was sparked when he saw microscopic organisms such as these with his toy microscope.

he might be a concert musician someday. Then, when he was eight or nine years old, Mario looked at a drop of water through a toy microscope. To his amazement, he saw a swarm of tiny creatures that were invisible without the microscope. Mario was dazzled. He yearned to know more and more about the natural world. His aunt, Esther Molina, was a chemist. She encouraged his growing interest in science. With her help, Mario turned a little-used bathroom in his family's large house into a chemistry laboratory.

Mario spent hour upon hour in his makeshift lab. Sometimes he studied everyday substances such as glue, plastic, and paint. He tried to discover the chemical **components** of them. Other times, he combined chemicals to create new substances. His family got used to the strange smells that wafted through the house. Mario's Aunt Esther often helped him plan and conduct experiments. He wished that his friends from school would help, too, but they preferred to play games in the park. None of his friends understood his excitement about science.

At age 11, Mario left home to attend a boarding school in faraway Switzerland. Though it was frightening

Mario Molina first left home to attend boarding school in Switzerland. Since then he has traveled to many different countries around the world to study and conduct research.

Young Molina traveled to Switzerland in the 1950s, at about the same time this photograph was taken.

to leave his family and friends, Mario was eager to go. Perhaps he would find new friends who loved science as much as he did. To his disappointment, the students at the Swiss school were much like the boys and girls he had known in Mexico City. To them, science was just another class they had to take. "My studies in chemistry were a lonely adventure," Molina recalled years later.

None of his classmates at the Swiss boarding school spoke Spanish, either. But several of them came from Italy, and Mario discovered that Spanish and Italian had much in common. He made friends with the Italian students and quickly learned their language. Since classes were taught in German, he mastered German as well.

After two years in Switzerland, Mario returned to Mexico to attend high school. In 1960, he entered UNAM to study **chemical engineering.** Again he hoped to find other students who had a passion for science. Once more, he was disappointed. The engineering students were interested in solving problems, but they didn't have Mario's endless curiosity. Unlike Mario, they didn't learn for the sheer joy of learning. Mario wondered if he would be on a lonely adventure for the rest of his life.

Chapter Two

Sharing the Adventure

After he graduated from UNAM, Mario Molina decided to continue his education in **physical chemistry.** Molina hoped that he would eventually study at a university in the United States. But he knew that first he needed to improve his skills in mathematics and several other important subjects. For this reason, he enrolled in courses at the University of Freiberg in Germany.

After nearly two years in Germany, he moved to Paris, France. There, Molina met a group of intelligent, talented young people. He quickly learned to talk with them in French. His new friends included artists and writers as well as scientists and mathematicians. Molina and his friends spent many happy hours in sidewalk cafes, talking about everything from art and politics to the meaning of life.

This building is located on the campus of the University of California at Berkeley. Molina describes his years at the school as among the best of his life.

In 1968, Molina entered a doctoral program in physical chemistry at the University of California at Berkeley. He knew very little English when he arrived, but he learned the language quickly as he plunged into his studies. Berkeley had students from around the world, and Molina made friends with many people from other countries.

One of his new friends was a chemistry student named Luisa Tan. She was a young woman of Chinese heritage who had grown up in the Philippines. When Molina found out that Luisa had never learned to drive, he offered to give her a lesson. As he sat beside her

Mario Molina and Luisa Tan are more than just husband and wife—they are also partners in scientific research. Both scientists have often worked on the same research team and have conducted several important experiments related to the atmosphere.

in the passenger seat, giving her directions and encouragement, she got into a minor accident. The accident dented the car but in no way damaged their budding romance. Mario Molina and Luisa Tan were married in July 1973.

At Berkeley, Molina discovered the community he had always longed for. His fellow students were deeply interested in pure science. They were driven by their curiosity and their desire to understand the workings of the natural world. Molina found it thrilling to be surrounded by people who shared his passion. He was no longer working alone.

One of Molina's teachers at Berkeley was named George C. Pimentel. Pimentel had discovered chemical lasers in the mid-1960s. A chemical laser is a powerful light beam produced by a **chemical reaction.** While studying with Pimentel, Molina began to do research on chemical lasers. Molina's research helped explain more fully how these lasers work. For the first time, Molina was making his own contribution to scientific knowledge.

Molina knew that chemical lasers could be used to create weapons. He wanted to do research that would benefit humankind, not research that would be used to harm people. Nevertheless, he believed that all scientific knowledge has value. Pure science, as he saw it, is neither good nor bad. Human beings can choose to use knowledge for good purposes or for evil purposes.

Mario Molina received his doctoral degree, or Ph.D., from the University of California at Berkeley in 1972. He stayed on at the Berkeley campus for another year, continuing his research. In the fall of 1973, he moved to

Molina later said that George C. Pimentel (shown speaking during a news conference) was an inspiring teacher who encouraged him to "pursue more important scientific questions." Pimentel began teaching at Berkeley in 1949 and remained there until his death 40 years later.

Irvine, California, to work under Professor F. Sherwood (Sherry) Rowland. Rowland suggested several areas of research that Molina might find interesting. The one that caught Molina's attention involved chemicals called **chlorofluorocarbons,** or CFCs. CFCs were produced by humans in the manufacture of **aerosol** sprays, refrigerants (cooling agents), and certain packaging materials.

Rowland wondered what became of CFCs once they entered Earth's atmosphere. Molina had worked with similar chemicals at Berkeley, but he had little background in the chemistry of the atmosphere.

As he discussed the project with Rowland, Molina saw that it would be a big challenge. But he also realized that it would be an opportunity to learn a great deal. He decided to make CFCs the focus of his new research.

Since F. Sherwood Rowland (shown here) spent part of 1974 in Vienna, Austria, he and Molina conducted much of their early research together by mail and telephone.

18

The word *laser* comes from the first letters in the phrase "*l*ight *a*mplification by *s*timulated *e*mission of *r*adiation." A laser is an intense beam of light that can be directed at a specific target. Doctors use lasers to cut through tissue during surgery. In mines deep beneath the earth's surface, laser beams can be used to drill through rock. Lasers may someday be used by the military to destroy missiles.

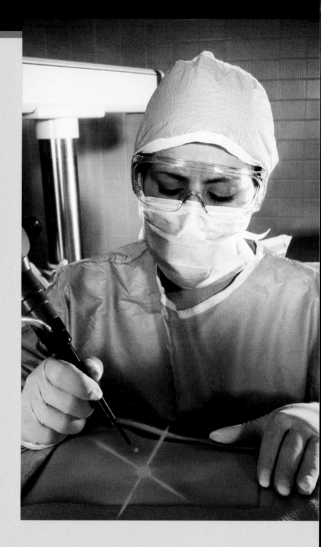

The first lasers were produced by electricity during the 1950s. In 1965, George C. Pimentel and other scientists discovered a way to produce lasers fueled by chemical reactions. Pimentel found that the reaction between two gases, hydrogen and fluorine, can produce enormously powerful light energy. Oxygen and iodine, mixed with the help of high-intensity sound waves, can also create lasers. Today, scientists are working to produce lasers more cleanly and efficiently.

Chapter Three

The Hidden Menace

When Mario Molina and Sherry Rowland began their research on CFCs in the atmosphere, no one was very worried about the subject. In the lower atmosphere, close to the ground, CFC **molecules** drift about harmlessly. Eventually, however, they float above the clouds to the upper atmosphere, or stratosphere. The CFCs that make it to the stratosphere are broken apart by the sun's rays.

The chemicals do not simply disappear, however. The sunlight breaks the CFCs into their basic components. One of these components is chlorine, a greenish-yellow gas. Molina and Rowland quickly realized that the chlorine atoms attacked and destroyed a chemical necessary for the health of plants, animals, and humans. That vital chemical is called ozone.

Ozone is a type of oxygen found between 8 and 30 miles (12 and 48 kilometers) above Earth's surface.

It forms a shield that protects the earth from the sun's dangerous ultraviolet rays. These ultraviolet rays can cause cancer and other diseases. Rowland and Molina knew that a few chlorine atoms could destroy tens of thousands of ozone molecules. They realized that as the number of CFCs in the atmosphere grew, the protective ozone layer would suffer more and more damage.

An inspector studies aerosol cans containing bug spray. CFCs were once found in cans of bug spray, hairspray, and paint.

Molina and Rowland were deeply concerned. They discussed their findings with atmospheric scientists at Berkeley. Those scientists were already aware that chlorine from other sources could damage the ozone layer. They had studied the effects of chlorine from volcanic eruptions and from fuel used in spacecraft. But they had not considered that CFCs could unleash chlorine in the stratosphere.

In 1928, scientists at the General Motors Company were looking for safe, inexpensive chemicals to act as cooling agents. They developed a new chemical **compound** that contained chlorine, fluorine, carbon, and hydrogen. This compound, known as a chlorofluorocarbon or CFC, was marketed under the name Freon. Freon was soon used in refrigerators and eventually in air conditioners. After World War II, manufacturers began to use other CFCs in aerosol (or spray-can) products such as hair sprays, insecticides, and paints.

Year after year, the production of CFCs around the world increased. Because CFCs are not poisonous to humans, their growing use aroused little concern. Until the early 1970s, no one suspected that they could damage the environment. Today, scientists know that CFCs that enter the atmosphere take between 50 and 140 years to break down.

In June 1974, Rowland and Molina published a report about their research in *Nature,* Great Britain's leading scientific journal. Scientists around the world read the article with interest. Molina and Rowland were invited to talk about their work at many scientific meetings. Yet they knew that speaking to scientists wasn't enough. To make a difference and protect the ozone layer, they had to convince the people who manufactured and used products containing CFCs of their danger.

In 1975, Molina and other scientists launched a massive effort to alert the public. In news stories and magazine articles, they described the impact of CFCs on the ozone layer. They met with government and corporate leaders. They worked to establish an international ban on CFCs.

Chlorine was released into the atmosphere when fuel was used to launch this rocket. But smaller, everyday products such as hairspray were also once responsible for damaging the ozone layer.

Before Molina conducted his experiments on CFCs, most people weren't aware of how average household items had a negative effect on the atmosphere. Today, people know more about the environment and are taking greater steps to protect it.

Little by little, people began to listen. In 1978, the United States, Canada, and several European nations agreed to ban the use of CFCs in aerosol sprays. Aerosol sprays accounted for about half the CFCs that reached the stratosphere. The ban was an important step, but Molina and others knew it didn't go far enough.

Then, in 1985, scientists in Antarctica made an alarming discovery. They found an enormous hole in the ozone layer above the South Pole. During the Antarctic winter, the hole was almost as big as the continental United States. It became smaller during the warmer summer season but grew again each winter. Molina helped explain what was happening. Clouds of ice **particles** over Antarctica hastened the ozone breakdown caused by CFCs in the atmosphere.

All over the world, headlines shouted the news about the hole in the ozone layer. Scientists warned that damage to the ozone layer could lead to crop failure and an increase in human cancer. These dire warnings terrified the public. Finally, both average citizens and government leaders understood that something had to be done. In 1987, most of the world's nations signed an agreement known as the Montreal Protocol. The Montreal Protocol carefully controls the manufacture and use of CFCs. With the help of this

This research station is located in Antarctica. The weather conditions in Antarctica allow certain gases to have an especially harmful effect on the ozone layer above that continent.

Chapter Four

A Call from Sweden

The Rogers Building is part of the campus at MIT. Molina began working at MIT in 1989, and he and his wife continue to conduct experiments there today.

One morning in 1995, as Mario Molina sat in his office at MIT, he received a long-distance telephone call. The caller explained that he was from the Royal Academy of Sciences in Stockholm, Sweden. Mario Molina had been awarded a Nobel Prize in chemistry.

Molina was astonished. He could hardly believe what he was hearing. This was the first time a Nobel Prize had been awarded for work on the effects of human-made

28

Paul Crutzen (left) receives his Nobel Prize in 1995. Crutzen currently works at a chemistry institute in Mainz, Germany.

chemicals. Molina was one of three Nobel Prize winners in chemistry that year. He and two other scientists who had also done important research on CFCs in the atmosphere shared the million-dollar prize. The other two winners were a German chemist, Paul Crutzen, and Molina's longtime friend and fellow researcher, F. Sherwood Rowland.

In Stockholm, on December 10, 1995, Mario Molina stood before the king and queen of Sweden to receive the Nobel Prize. Dr. Ingmar Grenthe of the Royal

Swedish Academy of Sciences introduced the winners with a short speech. "Professor Crutzen, Professor Molina, and Professor Rowland," he said, "You have . . . created a clearer understanding of fundamental chemical phenomena, [and] also of the large-scale and often negative consequences of human behavior. In the words of Alfred Nobel's will, your work has been of very great 'benefit to mankind.'"

Winning the Nobel Prize changed Molina's life. He was in constant demand to speak and write about his work. Universities and organizations showered him

Molina (center) speaks at a press conference shortly before receiving the Nobel Prize. On either side of him are fellow-winners F. Sherwood Rowland (left) and Paul Crutzen (right).

When the Swedish inventor, chemist, and businessman Alfred Nobel died in 1896, he left behind a large fortune. In his will, he declared that every year, money from his estate should be used to give prizes to those who "have conferred the greatest benefit to mankind." Nobel's will stated that prizes should be given in the fields of chemistry, physics, medicine, and literature. He also set up a Nobel Peace Prize to be awarded to a person who helped promote world peace. Later, a prize in economics was added to the list. Persons from any country in the world are eligible to win these awards. Nobel wanted only to make sure that "the most worthy shall receive the prize." Today, the Nobel Prize is one of the highest honors a person can receive. Through his will, Alfred Nobel left a gift for future generations.

This fertilizer plant in Brazil is releasing harmful chemicals into the atmosphere. Luckily, many countries now conduct inspections of factories such as the one shown here. Inspectors try to make sure that companies are doing everything possible to prevent poisonous chemicals from affecting the atmosphere.

with honors. For Molina, the Nobel Prize also carried great responsibilities. He wanted to use his growing renown to educate the public. CFCs were not the only chemicals that threatened the atmosphere. Molina believed that he must warn people about other human-made hazards that continue to pollute the air we breathe. He encouraged scientists, corporate leaders, and lawmakers to talk to each other about cleaning up the atmosphere.

Air pollution is a very severe problem in Mexico and other poor countries. Cars, buses, and factories pour tons of poisonous chemicals into the air each year. Few laws control the production of these chemicals. Those laws that do exist are seldom enforced. Molina saw a need to train students from poorer countries in the field of atmospheric chemistry. In 1996, he donated $200,000— nearly two-thirds of his Nobel Prize money—to MIT. He asked that the money be used to help students from poor nations around the world conduct research in atmospheric science.

The problem of air pollution is obvious in Mexico City. By the mid-1960s, the snowcapped peaks of Popocatepetl and Ixtacihuatl could no longer be seen from downtown. The towering mountains were

When scientists note that ozone levels are especially bad in Mexico City, government officials take emergency measures. In these instances, leaders might temporarily close fuel stations or factories, or even set a limit on the number of cars that can be driven!

As this train burns coal, a thick cloud of black smoke and soot is released into the atmosphere. Some scientists suspect that soot may have a harmful effect on the ozone layer.

hidden by clouds of smog. In 2000, Molina helped launch a project to improve Mexico City's air quality. Like many experts, he believes that Mexico City is a model for many cities of the future. Molina and his colleagues hope that scientists and city planners can learn from the Mexico City project. Then they can apply what they learn to projects in other cities. Maybe someday the people of Mexico City will again be able to gaze up from their balconies at the lovely peaks of Popocatepetl and Ixtacihuatl.

Molina continues to teach and do research at MIT. In recent years, he has been studying soot and its effects.

Soot is produced when wood and fossil fuels such as oil and coal are burned. Molina is studying the chemical properties of soot particles and the impact of soot on the atmosphere.

Whether he is in Cambridge or Mexico City, Molina is surrounded by students and scientists from all around the globe. He is among men and women who share his passion to unlock the mysteries of the natural world. He is always pleased to meet young people who care about the environment and want to keep it healthy. "Science is fascinating," he tells young people. "It's far more than homework and taking tests at school. Sometimes you have to discover a fascination with science in spite of the way it's taught in the classroom. Read, observe, and experiment on your own. We need many more scientists. We need many more young people with curiosity."

Because of Mario Molina's research, people are now more aware of how fragile our environment is, and of why it's so important to take better care of it. Perhaps his future studies will unlock even more ways to preserve the atmosphere.

1943: Mario Molina is born in Mexico City on March 19.

1954: Mario Molina leaves home to attend a boarding school in Switzerland.

1960: Molina enters the University of Mexico to study chemical engineering.

1965: Molina earns a degree in chemical engineering and decides he wants to obtain a degree in physical chemistry.

1967: Molina earns a postgraduate degree from the University of Freiberg in West Germany.

1968: Molina enrolls at the University of California at Berkeley.

1972: Molina earns his Ph.D.

1973: Molina and Luisa Tan are married. Molina takes a position at the University of California at Irvine.

1974: Molina and F. Sherwood Rowland publish a paper in the journal *Nature* about CFCs and the ozone layer.

1975: Molina becomes an assistant professor at UC Irvine. He and other scientists launch a massive effort to alert the public to the damage CFCs are causing.

1977: Mario and Luisa's son, Felipe, is born.

1978: The United States, Canada, and several European nations agree to ban the use of CFCs in aerosol sprays.

1982: Molina takes a job at the Jet Propulsion Laboratory at the California Institute of Technology.

1985: Scientists discover a hole in the ozone layer above Antarctica.

1987: Most of the world's nations sign the Montreal Protocol, limiting the manufacture and use of CFCs.

1989: Molina accepts a teaching position at the Massachusetts Institute of Technology (MIT).

1995: Molina and two other scientists win the Nobel Prize in chemistry for their work on CFCs and the ozone layer.

1996: Molina donates $200,000 of his Nobel Prize Money to MIT.

2000: Molina helps launch a project to improve the air quality of Mexico City.

2002: Molina and his wife publish *Air Quality in the Mexico Megacity*.

aerosol (AIR-uh-sawl) Aerosols are products made of fine particles that are dispensed from a spray can. Many aerosol sprays were banned after it was discovered that they damaged the ozone layer.

atmosphere (AT-muhs-fear) The atmosphere is the layer of gases surrounding the earth, including the air we breathe. Mario Molina studies the effects of human-made chemicals on the atmosphere.

chemical engineering (KEM-uh-kul en-juh-NEAR-ing) Chemical engineering is a science in which chemistry is used in industry. Mario Molina studied chemical engineering in college.

chemical reaction (KEM-uh-kul ree-AK-shun) A chemical reaction is the process by which the composition of chemicals changes when they interact. The chemical reaction between hydrogen and fluorine can produce a chemical laser.

chlorofluorocarbons (klore-oh-floor-oh-KAR-buns) Chlorofluorocarbons are chemical compounds that contain chlorine, fluorine, carbon, and hydrogen. The use of chlorofluorocarbons (CFCs) can damage the ozone layer.

components (kum-POH-nunts) Components are parts or ingredients. Chlorine is the component of CFCs that can damage the ozone layer.

compound (KOM-pound) A compound is a substance composed of two or more chemicals bonded together. Water is a compound made of hydrogen and oxygen.

molecules (MOL-uh-kyools) Molecules are the smallest possible pieces of a substance. The sun's rays break CFC molecules into their basic components, including chlorine, a poisonous gas.

particles (PAR-ti-kulz) Particles are tiny pieces or fragments. Mario Molina is studying how soot particles affect the atmosphere.

physical chemistry (FIZ-ih-kul KEM-uh-stree) Physical chemistry is the study of the chemical makeup of nonliving things. Mario Molina enrolled at the University of California at Berkeley to study physical chemistry.

Books

Cefrey, Holly. *What If the Hole in the Ozone Layer Gets Bigger?* Danbury, Conn.: Children's Press, 2002.

Donald, Rhonda Lucas. *The Ozone Layer.* Danbury, Conn.: Children's Press, 2002.

Pringle, Laurence P. *Vanishing Ozone: Protecting Earth from Ultraviolet Radiation.* New York: Morrow, 1995.

Web Sites

Visit our Web page for lots of links about Mario Molina:
http://www.childsworld.com/links.html

Note to parents, teachers, and librarians: We routinely check our Web links to make sure they're safe, active sites—so encourage your readers to check them out!

About the Author

Deborah Kent grew up in Little Falls, New Jersey, and received her bachelor's degree from Oberlin College. She earned a master's degree from Smith College School for Social Work and worked as a social worker before becoming a full-time writer. She is the author of 18 young-adult novels and more than 50 nonfiction titles for children. She lives in Chicago with her husband, children's author R. Conrad Stein, and their daughter, Janna.

Index

aerosol sprays, 18, *21,* 22, *22,* 24, *24*

Air Quality in the Mexico Megacity
  (Mario and Luisa Molina), 6

Antarctica, 24, *25*

California Institute of Technology, 27,
  27

chemical engineering, 13

chemical lasers, 16–17, 19, *19*

chemical reactions, 16–17, 19

chlorine gas, 20, 21, *23*

chlorofluorocarbons (CFCs), 18, 20,
  21, 22, 23, 24, 29

Crutzen, Paul, 29, *29, 30*

Freon, 22, *22*

General Motors Company, 22

Grenthe, Ingmar, 29–30

Jet Propulsion Laboratory (JPL), 27, *27*

lasers, 16–17, 19, *19*

map, *11*

Massachusetts Institute of Technology
  (MIT), 27, *28,* 33, 34

Mexico City, Mexico, 6, *7,* 33, *33*

microscopic organisms, 10, 10

Molina, Esther (aunt), 10

Molina, Felipe (son), 27

Molina, Luisa Tan (wife), 6, 15–16,
  16, 26–27

Molina, Mario, *16, 30, 35*
  birth of, 6
  childhood of, 8, 10
  education of, 10–11, 13, 14, 15, 16–17

as Nobel Prize recipient, 6, 28–30, 32
  as teacher, 26, 27

Molina Pasquel, Roberto (father), 6–7

Montreal Protocol, 25

Mount Ixtacihuatl, 8, *8,* 9, 33–34

Mount Popocatepetl, 8, 9, 33–34

Nature (scientific journal), 23

Nobel, Alfred, 31, *31*

Nobel Prizes, 6, 28–30, *29,* 31

ozone layer, 20–21, 23, 24–25, *26*

physical chemistry, 14

Pimentel, George C., 16, *17,* 19

pollution, 32, *32,* 33, *33, 34*

Rogers Building (MIT), *28*

Rowland, F. Sherwood "Sherry," 18,
  18, 20, 21, 23, 29, *30*

Royal Swedish Academy of Sciences,
  29–30

soot, 34–35, *34*

South Pole, 24, *25*

spacecraft, 21, *23*

stratosphere, 20, 21

Tenochtitlán, 9, *9*

ultraviolet rays, 21

University of California (Berkeley),
  15, *15,* 16–17, 21

University of Freiberg, 14

University of Mexico, 7, 13

volcanoes, 8, *8,* 21, 33–34